Why Are Polar Bears in Danger?

Written by Cam Gregory

Environmental Issues

Vital Vocabulary

die 14

drown 10

Polar bears are in danger,
because Earth is warming up.
When Earth warms up,
the pack ice melts.
It breaks up.

The pack ice melts and breaks as it warms up.

Polar bears live on the pack ice.
They eat seals.
The seals come up holes
in the ice.
Polar bears eat them
when they come up.

This polar bear is eating seal meat.

Big chunks of pack ice break off.
Some polar bears
are on the chunks of ice.
There are no seals to eat.
The polar bears are hungry.

This polar bear is on a chunk of ice.

Some polar bears swim
back to the pack ice.
It is too far.
Some polar bears drown.

This polar bear is swimming back to the pack ice.

If there is no pack ice,
there are no seals
for polar bears to eat.
They starve.

This polar bear
is starving

Some polar bears die.

polar bears
drown

polar bears
starve

polar bears
hungry

polar bears die

ice breaks up

Critical Thinking

What is happening in this photo?
What do you think will
happen next?